THE WORLD PRESS PRESENTS

YOU WERE BORN A CHAMPION... DON'T DIE A LOSER!

CHAMPION

The Secrets Of Great CHAMPIONS

J. Konrad Hölè

Proverbs 4:7 says, "Wisdom is the Principle
thing." Wisdom is the only proof that you are
being **"Mentored"** by the **"Most Intelligent
Person In The Universe,"** the "Holy Spirit."

Unless otherwise indicated, all Scripture quotations
are taken from the King James Version of the Bible.

Greatest Secrets of a Champion

Copyright © 1996 by J. Konrad Hölè
ISBN 1-888-696-02-8
World Centre Ministries
P.O. Box 41010
Minneapolis, MN 55441

Published by
The World Press
P.O. Box 41010
Minneapolis, MN 55441

Foreword

I realized that the closer I became to the **"Holy Spirit,"** who is the **"Spirit of Wisdom,"** not only would He teach me everything He knows, but He would ignite a craving within me to know more. You will never remember someone's **"Words,"** as much as you will remember someone's **"Point."** That is why I wrote this book. It is simply because I believe that one **"Diamond Key"** of wisdom can unlock a **"Vaulted Treasure"** of information.

You and I are only ever **"One Truth"** away from what we do not understand, and what we need to know. These are not copies of someone else's quotes, or revelation. These are **"Diamonds of Revelation"** that the "Holy Spirit" has unlocked to me in Crusades, Seminars, and Teachings around the world. Feel free to share these with someone that needs to know what you know.

Diamonds are not just a **"Girl's Bestfriend,"** they're everybody's **"BESTFRIEND."**

Enjoy.

J. Konrad

Dedication

Champions are not those who never get knocked down, they are simply those who decided not to stay down.

The ability to become a Champion is not determined by what others tell you, you can be, but by what you tell yourself you can be.

To everyone in professions, and divine backgrounds, who has, or will ever pay the price for success, this book is dedicated to you!

May you always know that you were created to WIN!

Love,

1

CHAMPIONS Move Beyond Where LOSERS Choose To Stay.

❶ The difference between coping and conquering, is in how much you settle for.

❷ Never become so comfortable with where you are, that you make no plans to go further.

❸ *God* can enter through the trap door of a mistake, and lead you to the place He was unable to lead you prior to that point.

─── W i n n i n g   W o r d s ───

By much slothfulness the building decayeth; and through idleness of the hands the house droppeth through.
Ecclesiastes 10:18

2

CHAMPIONS Strategize, LOSERS Criticize.

❶ Jealous people are those who have become more side tracked with where you are, than where they could be.

❷ Those not making suggestions for your improvements, are disqualified from criticizing your achievements.

❸ You will only keep your successes as long as you keep your focus.

— W i n n i n g   W o r d s —

Having a good conscience; that, whereas they speak evil of you, as of evildoers, they may be ashamed that falsely accuse... I Peter 3:16

3

CHAMPIONS Are Motivated, By What LOSERS Are Intimidated By.

1 Inferiority that is motivated, is greater than superiority that is complacent.

2 The more afraid you are to be yourself, the less afraid you'll be of being someone else.

3 The only walls that stop you, will be the ones you build yourself.

Winning Words

Be strong and of a good courage, fear not, nor be afraid of them: for the LORD thy God, he it is that doth go with thee; he will not fail thee, nor forsake thee.   Deuteronomy 31:6

4

CHAMPIONS
Learn From
Their Past,
LOSERS Live
In It.

◆ Your enemy uses your past for "Condemnation," *God* uses your past for "Revelation."

◆ When you look behind, you fall behind.

◆ It's not temporary offenses that kill you, but rather your permanent attachment to them that does.

W i n n i n g   W o r d s

Brethren, I count not myself to have apprehended: but this one thing I do, forgetting those things which are behind, and reaching forth unto those things which are before,   Philippians 3:13

4

5

CHAMPIONS Make Improvements, LOSERS Make Excuses.

◆ *God* will always change you to greater, never average.

◆ Improvements are only as quick as your ability to recognize deficiency.

◆ You will not succeed in your future, how you are in your present, so *God* makes changes along the way.

Winning Words

Being confident of this very thing, that he which hath begun a good work in you will perform it until the day of Jesus Christ: Philippians 1:6

5

6

CHAMPIONS
Pursue, What
LOSERS
Wait For.

❶ You will never possess something, until the pursuit of going after it overwhelms the passivity of living without it.

❷ Never stop the movement towards your future, by self defending your present.

❸ Never ask *God* to give you something you are unwilling to go after.

W i n n i n g   W o r d s

For every one that asketh receiveth; and he that seeketh findeth; and to him that knocketh it shall be opened.
Matthew 7:8

7

CHAMPIONS Confront What LOSERS Complain About.

1️⃣ Those who complain about problems, rarely find solutions.

2️⃣ Promotion is not for those who point out problems, it's for those who solve them.

3️⃣ Complacency never starts "Big," it begins small, and gains momentum.

Winning Words

Without counsel purposes are disappointed: but in the multitude of counsellors they are established.
Proverbs 15:22

8

CHAMPIONS Speak Plainly, LOSERS Speak Politically.

◆ Your words determine the level of change peoples lives experience.

◆ If something has no point, it has no purpose.

◆ Accurate words leave you elevated above hearsay. Inaccurate words leave you obligated to damage control.

────── W i n n i n g   W o r d s ──────

Hear; for I will speak of excellent things; and the opening of my lips shall be right things. Proverbs 8:6

9

CHAMPIONS "Test," LOSERS Trust.

❶ Those you become linked to, are those you will imitate.

❷ Time interrogates other peoples promises, until believability emerges.

❸ Patience will offend those not permitted to manipulate you with haste.

Winning Words

But let patience have her perfect work, that ye may be perfect and entire, wanting nothing. James 1:4

10

CHAMPIONS Are Efficient, LOSERS Are Complacent.

❶ Others will notice your effort to be excellent, more than your acceptance to be mediocre.

❷ Excellence will cost you, what mediocrity will save you.

❸ It's not until you get on the battlefield, that you realize how relaxed you became in the palace.

Winning Words

In all things showing thyself a pattern of good works: in doctrine showing uncorruptness, gravity, sincerity, Titus 2:7

11

CHAMPIONS
Change What
LOSERS
Defend.

◆ Never be so loyal to a wrong decision that you refuse to let repentance reverse it.

◆ You cannot change error, until you can recognize it.

◆ God does not change you to make you miserable, but to make you effective.

Winning Words

*And thine ears shall hear a word behind thee, saying,
This is the way, walk ye in it... Isaiah 30:21*

12

CHAMPIONS Embrace Truth, LOSERS Consider It.

◆ Never distort truth to gain favor.

◆ Those who embrace truth, will risk correction in order to find it.

◆ Those who embrace truth, have no tolerance for those who embrace error.

———— W i n n i n g   W o r d s ————

Howbeit when he, the Spirit of truth, is come, he will guide you into all truth: for he shall not speak of himself; but whatsoever he shall hear, that shall he speak: and he will show you things to come.   John 16:13

13

CHAMPIONS Have Plans, LOSERS Have Thoughts.

◆ Anything not written, is a thought not a plan.

◆ If you don't prepare to succeed, you will prepare to fail.

◆ If you don't have a goal, you'll never have a future.

─── W i n n i n g   W o r d s ───

For which of you, intending to build a tower, sitteth not down first, and counteth the cost, whether he have sufficient to finish it?   Luke 14:28

14

CHAMPIONS "Do," LOSERS "Talk."

◆ Truth is never evident, until it's applied.

◆ The difference between waiting and moving is information.

◆ Your words either say where you are staying or where you are going.

Winning Words

The soul of the sluggard desireth, and hath nothing:
but the soul of the diligent shall be made fat.
Proverbs 13:4

14

15

CHAMPIONS

Observe,

LOSERS

React.

◆ Whatever you can observe, you can understand. Whatever you can understand, you can master.

◆ Never answer something that has not been asked.

◆ Anothers leverage against you, is based on how they think you will react.

W i n n i n g   W o r d s

He that answereth a matter before he heareth it, it is folly and shame unto him.   Proverbs 18:13

16

CHAMPIONS
Fall Down,
LOSERS
Stay Down.

1 If you wait to release a tragedy until you can explain it, you will place your recovery on indefinite delay.

2 Failure is not final. It's a temporary delay, not a permanent defeat.

3 When man sees your failures, he sees your end.
When God sees your failures, He sees your beginning.

Winning Words

Though he fall, he shall not be utterly cast down: for the LORD upholdeth him with his hand. Psalms 37:24

17

CHAMPIONS Sacrifice Today To Create Tomorrow, LOSERS Sacrifice Tomorrow To Create Today.

1 You will never understand the power of "Short Term Decisions" until you put everything through the "Long Range Process."

2 Time keeps you where you are, long enough for God to supply the resources to stay, or the instructions to leave.

3 Impatience will place you in intentional situations, that miracles will be forced to bail you out of.

───────── W i n n i n g   W o r d s ─────────

For ye have need of patience, that, after ye have done the will of God, ye might receive the promise.   **Hebrews 10:36**

18
CHAMPIONS Emanate Who They Are, LOSERS Emanate Who They Are Not.

1. Confident people know who they are, insecure people prove who they are.

2. Quiet confidence supersedes loud insecurity.

3. The sale of your independence, is the last stage before obscurity.

— Winning Words —

I will praise thee; for I am fearfully and wonderfully made: marvellous are thy works; and that my soul knoweth right well.   Psalms 139:14

19

CHAMPIONS Seek Direction, LOSERS Seek Opinions.

1. If you don't believe in your vision, what others say about it will shake you.

2. Those that criticize where you're going, are incapable of giving you what you're going after.

3. Never defend where you are going, to those not going there.

─────── W i n n i n g   W o r d s ───────

Where there is no vision, the people perish: but he that keepeth the law, happy is he.   Proverbs 29:18

20
CHAMPIONS
See Adversity
As A Beginning,
LOSERS See
Adversity As
An End.

◆ Adversity is not an enemy, it's just the proof you have one.

◆ Adversity is used by your enemy as a "Crisis," and by God as a "Classroom."

◆ Success is not the immunity from adversity, it's the proof you conquered it.

───────── W i n n i n g   W o r d s ─────────

When thou passest through the waters, I will be with thee; and through the rivers, they shall not overflow thee: when thou walkest through the fire, thou shalt not be burned; neither shall the flame kindle upon thee.   Isaiah 43:2

21

CHAMPIONS Do What Is Right, LOSERS Do What Is Popular.

◆ Integrity will only develop in you, when the pain of your mistakes births enough conviction to silence repetition.

◆ Never gossip to gain acceptance.

◆ Connect with those who sharpen your integrity, not soothe your lack of it.

Winning Words

The just man walketh in his integrity: his children are blessed after him.   Proverbs 20:7

22

CHAMPIONS Choose A Side, LOSERS Choose An Escape.

◆ Be a voice for something, instead of silent for everything.

◆ Have enough fortitude to pick a side, and enough conviction to walk on it.

◆ You will never change anything you are incapable of hating.

Winning Words

Looking unto Jesus the author and finisher of our faith; who for the joy that was set before him endured the cross, despising the shame, and is set down at the right hand of the throne of God.   Hebrews 12:2

23

CHAMPIONS Learn From Mistakes, LOSERS Live With Them.

1 The pain of failure will stay with you, until the photograph of starting over supersedes it.

2 Those that can survive a crash, are greater than those that think they never will.

3 The strategy to replace a mistake, comes from the honesty to admit, "You made one."

─── W i n n i n g   W o r d s ───

Ye are of God, little children, and have overcome them: because greater is he that is in you, than he that is in the world.   I John 4:4

24

CHAMPIONS
Ask,
LOSERS
Presume.

◆ You must identify the information you need, before you can qualify the questions you need to get it.

◆ Those who never ask, never learn.

◆ Those who never interrogate greatness, never become great.

─── W i n n i n g   W o r d s ───

If any of you lack wisdom, let him ask of God, that giveth to all men liberally, and upbraideth not; and it shall be given him.   James 1:5

25

CHAMPIONS Multiply, LOSERS Nullify.

◆ Nothing is never multiplied unless it is managed.

◆ You will never gain by one, what you can only gain with several.

◆ Opposition is never present, until multiplication is possible.

Winning Words

Now he that ministereth seed to the sower both minister bread for your food, and multiply your seed sown, and increase the fruits of your righteousness; II Corinthians 9:10

26

CHAMPIONS Build Legacies, LOSERS Build Enemies.

❶ A successor is proof *God* did not intend for your mantle to die when you do.

❷ You will be remembered more for what you left, than what you did.

❸ Your life is a classroom for the next generation.

Winning   Words

When I call to remembrance the unfeigned faith that is in thee, which dwelt first in thy grandmother Lois, and thy mother Eunice; and I am persuaded that in thee also.
II Timothy 1:5

27

CHAMPIONS Will Complete What LOSERS Will Begin.

◆ You will never reach completion without a map to the finish line.

◆ Your assignment will either be promoted or distracted by a person.

◆ You will never have a platform for your achievements, until you have a fortress for your focus.

─── W i n n i n g   W o r d s ───

For the LORD shall be thy confidence, and shall keep thy foot from being taken.   Proverbs 3:26

28

CHAMPIONS Protect, LOSERS Propagate.

❶ Reward loyalty. If it doesn't become important, it may become absent.

❷ Those that do not guard others, will not guard you.

❸ The moment you can purchase loyalty, is the moment it can be sold for a higher price.

Winning Words

Faithful are the wounds of a friend; but the kisses of an enemy are deceitful.   Proverbs 27:6

29

CHAMPIONS
Interrogate,
LOSERS
Believe.

◆ The wise interrogate rumor, the ignorant believe it.

◆ You will never arrive at truth, until you go on an "Unbias Journey" to find it.

◆ If a persons words cannot survive interrogation, they are disqualified for consideration.

Winning   Words

Let us hear the conclusion of the whole matter: Fear God, and keep his commandments: for this is the whole duty of man.   Ecclesiastes 12:13

30

CHAMPIONS
Use Time,
LOSERS
Waste It.

1 Time is a universal currency. What you purchase with it, will determine your future.

2 Time interrogates possibility, until direction emerges.

3 Time allows revelation to repair failures.

W i n n i n g   W o r d s

To every thing there is a season, and a time to every purpose under the heaven: Ecclesiastes 3:1

30

31

CHAMPIONS Follow Integrity, LOSERS Follow Diplomacy.

◆ Integrity is practiced, diplomacy is proclaimed.

◆ Diplomacy is a harbor from the storms of commitment.

◆ The more that integrity flows through your life, the more unethical people will be uncomfortable around your life.

Clip & Mail

Let Me Agree With You In Prayer For Your Need!

You are daily upon my heart and your needs matter greatly to me. Don't ever think that you are alone. I want to agree with you that the Holy Spirit will bring the provision of God in your life!

_____

_____

_____

_____

_____

_____

_____

_____

_____

_____

_____

_____

_____

_____

Name _____

Address _____

City _____State _____Zip _____

Phone ( )_____

Clip & Mail To: Spirit & Life Ministries
P.O. BOX 41010   MINNEAPOLIS, MN 55441

Clip & Mail

"The Diamond Library For Achievers"
Several Dynamic Topics:

Build Your Complete Achiever Library!

Obedience
Join J. Konrad for this "Impactive" study on the "Power" of OBEDIENCE and its ability to be the bridge from "Where You Are," to "Where You Want To Be ," and God's ability to react to your life everytime you follow one of "His Instructions."
$10.00 (2 tapes)

Time
Join J. Konrad for this "Impactive" study on the "Currency of TIME," its ability to form your "Destiny" around you, and its critical role in developing your relationship with the Holy Spirit.
$10.00 (2 tapes)

Focus
Join J. Konrad for this "Impactive" study on the Force of "FOCUS," and its ability to enable you to walk through the "Valleys of Distraction," and complete your life assignment!
$10.00 (2 tapes)

Send Your Order In Today!

Seed-Faith
Join J. Konrad for this "Impactive" study on the "Power Of Seed Movement" in your life, and your ability to take something God has placed in your hand, to create something God has ordained in your life.
$10.00 (2 tapes)

Warfare
Join J. Konrad for this "Impactive" study of how you were not called to be a "Captive," you were called to be a "Deliverer."
$10.00 (2 tapes)

Direction
Join J. Konrad for this "Impactive" study on how the "HOLY SPIRIT" answers one of the most pivotal questions ever in your life... the question of DIRECTION.!
$10.00 (2 tapes)

SPECIAL PACKAGE PRICE... Receive all 6 titles into your life for just $30. (please specify when ordering)

More Power-Packed Teaching From J. Konrad Hölè

The Leading Of His Spirit

Join J. Konrad for this "Explosive" and "In-Depth" study on how the Holy Spirit leads you more by "Purpose, Principals and Protocal" than He does by Euphoria, Emotion, and Excitement. The greatest seasons of your life are just ahead, LED BY HIS SPIRIT.

$20.00 (4 tape series)

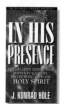

In His Presence

Find out the life changing secrets of Kind David's revelation of how to live in the Presence of God. The most incredible breakthroughs in your life are about to take place just be being in His Presence.

$15.00 (3 tape series)

Diary Of The Holy Spirit

Discover the benefits of how to Commune, Flow, Discern, and Listen to the Holy Spirit who Jesus said would be with you Always. Your greatest relationship is one revelation away.

$15.00 (3 tape series)

Misery

Discover David's revelation principles from Psalms 16:11, that the only true place of joy was in God's presence, and that anything outside His presence was not designed to satisfy you, but rather would be a source of "Misery."

$20.00 (4 tape series)

The Mentor And The Protege

What is a *Mentor*? A gift by *God* to insure the success of completing your *Assignment*. What is a *Protege*? A person whose future depends on the impartation from somebody who has already been where they are going. In this impactive teaching you will understand the purpose of mentoring.

$20.00 (4 tape series)

*Don't let these opportunities pass you by! Rush
your order in today. Fill out the form below.
Please print clearly and legibly. Ask the Holy
Spirit what Seed He would have you to sow into
this world-changing ministry.*

Title	Qty.	Price	Total
The Leading Of His Spirit (Tapes)		$	$
In His Presence (Tapes)		$	$
The Diary Of The Holy Spirit (Tapes)		$	$
Misery (Tapes)		$	$
The Mentor And The Protege (Tapes)		$	$
Library For Achievers - Time (Tapes)		$	$
Library For Achievers - Obedience (Tapes)		$	$
Library For Achievers - Focus (Tapes)		$	$
Library For Achievers - Seed-Faith (Tapes)		$	$
Library For Achievers - Warfare (Tapes)		$	$
Library For Achievers - Direction (Tapes)		$	$

1 Item.....................$2 - S/H	Shipping/Handling	$
2 Items ....$3 - S/H	Seed-Faith Gift	$
3 or more Items.....$4 - S/H	**Total**	$

☐ J. Konrad, please send me my **FREE** copy of your *Spirit & Life
   Talk* newsletter.

☐ Check   ☐ Money Order   ☐ Visa   ☐ MasterCard

Card No. ☐☐☐☐☐☐☐☐☐☐☐☐☐☐☐☐☐☐☐☐

Exp. Date _____ Signature _____

Name _____

Address _____

City _____ State _____ Zip _____

Phone (_____)_____

Clip & Mail To: Spirit & Life Ministries
P.O. BOX 41010   MINNEAPOLIS, MN 55441

*Choose From These Exciting Titles! Books
that will bring a Breakthrough... Your life
will be challenged and changed with
revelation knowledge!*

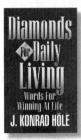

**Diamonds For
Daily Living**

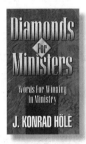

**Diamonds For
Ministers**

**Diamonds For
Mothers**

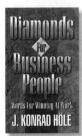

**Diamonds For
Business People**

**You Were Born A
Champion... Don't
Die A Loser!**

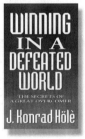

**Winning In A
Defeated World**

**Leading In the
Midst Of
Followers**

**Living Large In
A Small World**

**See the next
page for
details on how
to order your
personal
copies of
these books!**

"Literature Evangelism Team"

Order Form

☐ Yes, J. Konrad, I want to be a part of this "Evangelism Breakthrough" so that I may affect those that God links me to with the power of revelation knowledge.

Order a set of 10 copies of any title for $10. You may also mix titles of the books to bring a total of 10 copies for $10. Order for your friends and family!

Title	Qty. (Sets of 10)	Price	Total
Diamonds For Daily Living		x $10	$
Diamonds For Ministers		x $10	$
Diamonds For Mothers		x $10	$
Diamonds For Business People		x $10	$
You Were Born A Champion...		x $10	$
Winning In A Defeated World		x $10	$
Leading In The Midst Of Followers		x $10	$
Living Large In A Small World		x $10	$
Add $2 For Shipping	Shipping		$
	Seed-Faith Gift		$
	Total		$

☐ Check ☐ Money Order ☐ Visa ☐ MasterCard

Card No. ⬚⬚⬚⬚⬚⬚⬚⬚⬚⬚⬚⬚⬚⬚⬚⬚

Exp. Date _____ Signature _____

Name _____

Address _____

City _____ State _____ Zip _____

Phone (___) _____

Clip & Mail To: Spirit & Life Ministries
P.O. BOX 41010   MINNEAPOLIS, MN 55441